The Pied Piper of Hamelin

First published in 2005 by
Franklin Watts
96 Leonard Street
London
EC2A 4XD

Franklin Watts Australia
45–51 Huntley Street
Alexandria
NSW 2015

A CIP catalogue record for this book is available
from the British Library.

ISBN 0 7496 6152 6 (hbk)
ISBN 0 7496 6164 X (pbk)

Series Editor: Jackie Hamley
Series Advisor: Dr Barrie Wade
Series Designer: Peter Scoulding

Printed in Hong Kong / China

The Pied Piper of Hamelin

Retold by Anne Adeney

Illustrated by Jan Lewis

FRANKLIN WATTS
LONDON • SYDNEY

Once upon a time, there
was a town called Hamelin.

Hamelin was a fine town,
but it had a big
problem.

Rats! There were rats
everywhere!

Rats bit the babies.

They ate up every scrap
of food.

Something had to be done. A strange man came to Hamelin.

"I am the Pied Piper,"
said the strange man.

"I can get rid of all
your rats."

"First you must promise to pay me," the Pied Piper said.

gnats ~ 1 bag of gold
mice ~ 2 bags of gold
rats ~ 3 bags of gold
vampire bats ~ 4 bags of gold
snakes ~ 5 bags of gold
Dragons ~ 10 bags of gold

The people promised to
pay the Pied Piper three
bags of gold.

The Pied Piper began
to play his pipe.

His magic music made all the rats follow him.

20

They danced to his tune
down to the river.

The rats were never seen in Hamelin again. The people were so happy!

23

But they did not pay the
gold they had promised.

The Pied Piper was
very angry.

He began to play his
pipe again.

This time, his magic music made all the children follow him.

They danced to his tune
up to the mountains and
into a wonderful kingdom.
Only one boy could
not keep up.

The children were never
seen again. After that,
the sad people of
Hamelin always
kept their promises.

Leapfrog has been specially designed to fit the requirements of the National Literacy Strategy. It offers real books for beginning readers by top authors and illustrators.

There are 31 Leapfrog stories to choose from:

The Bossy Cockerel
Written by Margaret Nash, illustrated by Elisabeth Moseng

Bill's Baggy Trousers
Written by Susan Gates, illustrated by Anni Axworthy

Mr Spotty's Potty
Written by Hilary Robinson, illustrated by Peter Utton

Little Joe's Big Race
Written by Andy Blackford, illustrated by Tim Archbold

The Little Star
Written by Deborah Nash, illustrated by Richard Morgan

The Cheeky Monkey
Written by Anne Cassidy, illustrated by Lisa Smith

Selfish Sophie
Written by Damian Kelleher, illustrated by Georgie Birkett

Recycled!
Written by Jillian Powell, illustrated by Amanda Wood

Felix on the Move
Written by Maeve Friel, illustrated by Beccy Blake

Pippa and Poppa
Written by Anne Cassidy, illustrated by Philip Norman

Jack's Party
Written by Ann Bryant, illustrated by Claire Henley

The Best Snowman
Written by Margaret Nash, illustrated by Jörg Saupe

Eight Enormous Elephants
Written by Penny Dolan, illustrated by Leo Broadley

Mary and the Fairy
Written by Penny Dolan, illustrated by Deborah Allwright

The Crying Princess
Written by Anne Cassidy, illustrated by Colin Paine

Jasper and Jess
Written by Anne Cassidy, illustrated by François Hall

The Lazy Scarecrow
Written by Jillian Powell, illustrated by Jayne Coughlin

The Naughty Puppy
Written by Jillian Powell, illustrated by Summer Durantz

Freddie's Fears
Written by Hilary Robinson, illustrated by Ross Collins

Cinderella
Written by Barrie Wade, illustrated by Julie Monks

The Three Little Pigs
Written by Maggie Moore, illustrated by Rob Hefferan

Jack and the Beanstalk
Written by Maggie Moore, illustrated by Steve Cox

The Three Billy Goats Gruff
Written by Barrie Wade, illustrated by Nicola Evans

Goldilocks and the Three Bears
Written by Barrie Wade, illustrated by Kristina Stephenson

Little Red Riding Hood
Written by Maggie Moore, illustrated by Paula Knight

Rapunzel
Written by Hilary Robinson, illustrated by Martin Impey

Snow White
Written by Anne Cassidy, illustrated by Melanie Sharp

The Emperor's New Clothes
Written by Karen Wallace, illustrated by François Hall

The Pied Piper of Hamelin
Written by Anne Adeney, illustrated by Jan Lewis

Hansel and Gretel
Written by Penny Dolan, illustrated by Graham Philpot

The Sleeping Beauty
Written by Margaret Nash, illustrated by Barbara Vagnozzi